SCIENCE IN ACTION

Fossils

Written by John Stidworthy

CHERRYTREE BOOKS

A Cherrytree Book

Designed and produced by Templar Publishing Ltd,
Pippbrook Mill, London Road, Dorking, Surrey RH4 1JE

First published 1989
by Cherrytree Press Ltd,
a subsidiary of
The Chivers Company Ltd,
Windsor Bridge Road,
Bath, Avon BA2 3AX

British Library Cataloguing in Publication Data

Stidworthy, John
    Fossils.
    1. Fossils. For schools
    I. Title   II. Series
    560

    ISBN 0-7451-5035-7   91-107

Printed and bound by L.E.G.O., Vicenza, Italy

PICTURE CREDITS
Key: Top = t, bottom = b

Front cover: S Stammers / Science Photo Library

Page 6-7: L Parry / RIDA
Page 9: Soames Summerhays / Science Photo Library
Page 13: GSF Picture Library
Page 16-17: GSF Picture Library / Yale University
Page 20: GSF Picture Library
Page 21: David Bayliss / RIDA
Page 24-25: Rex Features
Page 27 t: R T J Moody / RIDA
Page 27 b: GSF Picture Library
Page 28 & 29: GSF Picture Library
Page 30 & 31 t: GSF Picture Library
Page 31 b: Sinclair Stammers / RIDA
Page 32 t: RIDA
Page 33: GSF Picture Library
Page 36-37: Richard Moody / RIDA
Page 40 t: GSF Picture Library
Page 40 b: Eric & David Hosking

Artwork by: Tony Gibbons / Bernard Thornton Artists
              Sallie Reason

CONTENTS

GOLDEN RULES

This book contains a number of projects and things to try for yourself to help you find out more about the remains of animals or plants that died millions of years ago. These remains are called *fossils*. They have been preserved by being buried in rocks.

▶ Scientists known as *palaeontologists* have gathered together many facts about life in the past by studying fossils. Few fossils are complete and easy to study. Studying fossils is like detective work. If by chance you find the right fossil, it may give you a fascinating piece of information about the story of the Earth.

Amateur fossil hunters have made some very exciting finds in the past. If you find a fossil that you think may be important, be sure to take it to your local museum.

▶ As you will be an active scientist, it's a good idea to start collecting for your laboratory. Nearly everything you need can be found around your home. Bottles and jars will often be used, so when you see useful containers being thrown away, wash them up, and store them away.

■ GOOD SCIENTISTS...

ALWAYS THINK SAFETY FIRST

Let your parents know what you are doing. Do not put yourself in danger to collect fossils. Do not hammer at the faces of cliffs or quarries. Rocks may fall from above. Make sure you know the time of high tide so that you do not get cut off by the tide at seaside cliffs.

ALWAYS KEEP A NOTEBOOK

Whatever you are doing, it is a good idea to keep notes as you go along, just as any scientist would. That way you have a clear record of what you did. It may also help you see what's happened if something goes wrong or does not work.

ALWAYS FOLLOW THE COUNTRY CODE

Leave no litter. Keep to footpaths or field edges. Close gates behind you. Do not damage fences or walls. Do not disturb crops or livestock.

▶ In order to become a good detective, and a good scientist, there are a number of rules to follow. The experiments in this book should be safe if carried out properly, but some require equipment that could be dangerous if used carelessly. Make sure you read carefully what needs to be done before you actually do it. If you are not sure of anything, ask an adult for help or advice. When using sharp tools remember to ask an adult's permission and if you have any difficulties ask them to help you with the project.

▶ It will be useful to have a working surface near a sink that you can use for some of your work. Remember to clear up after you do an experiment. Throw away anything you will not use again. Clean the equipment you use ready for next time.

▶ When you go fossil collecting tell someone exactly where you are going, and what time you expect to be back. Go with a friend if you can. Do not forget to ask for permission if you are going on to private land. Always make sure that you do not go anywhere that looks dangerous.

NEVER GIVE UP TOO SOON

Do not be surprised or disappointed if something does not work exactly as it should. No two fossils and pieces of rock are identical, and what works well on one may not work on another. Sometimes fossils break just as you thought you were getting a perfect specimen.

NEVER PUT YOURSELF AT RISK

It is a good idea to protect your eyes with goggles when hammering rocks.

NEVER BE INCONSIDERATE

If you go to a quarry, you will need to get permission from the owner. Some owners refuse, or may lay down special conditions for safety reasons. You should also get permission from a landowner to go on his land to collect fossils.

WHAT IS A FOSSIL?

A fossil is the remains of an animal or plant that lived long ago. Most fossils are buried in *rocks* and are found when they are dug up. For a long time, people thought that they were remains of creatures drowned in the Biblical flood or the work of the Devil.

Gradually, scientists realized how rocks form. Ever since the Earth was formed, its rocky surface has been eroded, or worn away, by wind and water. If you watch waves crashing against a cliff you can almost see the rocks crumbling. Rock fragments and particles (*sediment*) are washed into rivers which carry them to the sea. There the sediment settles on the sea bed, builds up and slowly forms rock. More layers build up on top. In time, the sea level may drop and expose the rocks, or earth movements may lift the rocks above the sea.

Different layers, or ages, of rock contain different kinds of fossils. Plants and animals have changed over time. In the youngest rocks, many of the fossils are similar to living animals and plants. But in older rocks, the remains are of very different kinds of plants and animals. The oldest known rocks do not contain fossils.

The earliest fossil remains are of very simple animals and plants. Later fossils are of more complicated types. Some of the earlier kinds became *extinct*. This process of change of plants and animals over long periods of time is known as *evolution*.

Fossils can tell us about how living things have evolved. They can show us what life was like at a certain time in the past. They may even show what the

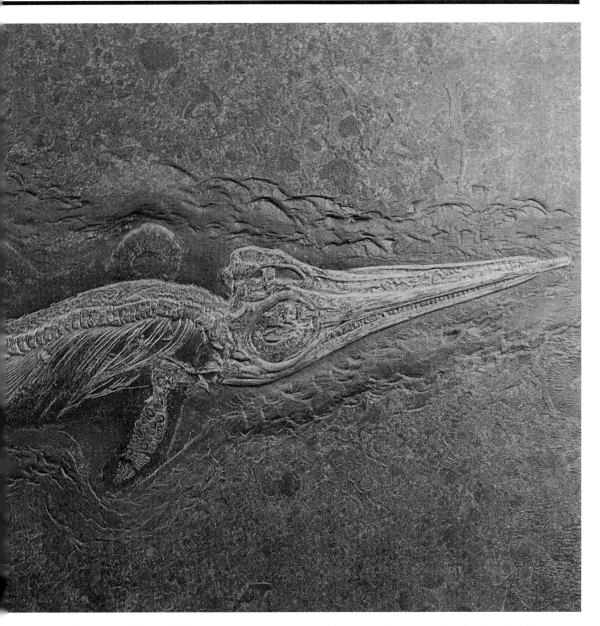

weather was like millions of years ago. But part of the fascination of fossils is that they can hardly ever tell the whole story. Often scientists can only guess at the way these animals lived. However, new fossils are being discovered all the time which help to unravel the mysteries of the Earth's past.

ROCK FORMATION

There are three main kinds of rock. *Igneous* rocks are formed from molten rock inside the earth. Sometimes the molten rock, called magma, cools underground. Later, earth movements may bring it to the surface. Igneous rocks are also formed when molten rock (lava) is thrown out by a volcano. Rocks such as granite and pumice are formed from the cooled lava. Fossils are rarely found in igneous rocks, except when a layer of volcanic ash comes down and buries an animal or plant.

Layer upon layer

The action of rain, wind and extremes of temperature erodes the surface of the Earth. Rock particles are washed away and carried down streams and rivers. When the rivers slow, as in an estuary, they can no longer carry the material along. The particles fall to the bottom as sediment. More and more fall, until those that fell first are squashed to form new rocks – *sedimentary rocks*. Most fossils are found in sedimentary rocks, which cover three-quarters of the Earth's land area.

SCIENCE PROJECT

Earth-shaking experiment

1   Put a couple of spoonfuls of garden soil in a jam jar. Now add a spoon or two of sand. Fill three-quarters of the jar with water. Put the lid on tight. Shake the jar hard for a minute. In the fast-moving water, the earth and sand will be suspended, as they would be in a fast-flowing river.

2   Stand the jar on a level table and leave it for a minute or two. What happens to the grains which were swirling in the water? Do they fall to the bottom in a jumble, or do separate layers form, one on top of the other? Are the biggest grains at the top, or at the bottom?

3   When sediment is deposited to form rock it works in this way too. If you have a piece of rock with several banded layers in it, you may be able to tell which way up it was originally by the size of the grains at the top and bottom of each layer.

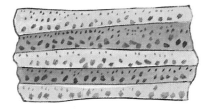

SCIENCE FACTFILE

Rocks are often moved or folded by movements in the Earth's crust. Along faults, or cracks in the Earth's crust, the land is raised up or forced down, exposing different layers, or strata, of rocks. Some movements of the Earth cause the Earth's crust to fold up in various ways to form outcrops. You can see these in sea cliffs. As the rocks are eroded, strata of different ages are exposed, and so different fossils come to light.

Two faults have pushed the rocks up (a) and down (b) exposing different layers of rock.

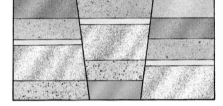

This is an anticline. As the rock erodes, the underlying layers will be exposed.

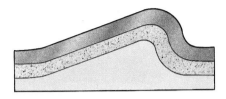

This is a syncline.

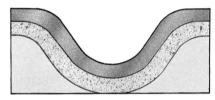

This is an overfold. On the underside the layers have turned upside down.

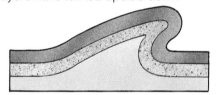

Reformed rocks

Occasionally, igneous or sedimentary rocks are violently compressed by earth movements or exposed to intense heat on the surface or within the Earth. Their structure and composition are changed, and *metamorphic* rock is formed – the third main kind of rock. Fossil remains are hard to find in such rocks because they are crushed, twisted or melted beyond recognition.

Erupting volcanoes throw out blazing-hot lava and ash.

HOW FOSSILS FORM

Sedimentary rocks throughout the world have been found to contain the fossilized remains of animals and plants. As fossils only form under special conditions, and changing conditions can destroy them, the fossil record of the Earth's history is incomplete.

Covered by sediment

As the rocky material, including mud and sand, is washed downstream by water, dead organisms are buried in it when it settles. As more layers of sediment build up, they are *preserved*. Most fossils are sea creatures, although remains of dead land animals and plants may also be swept down rivers, then dropped and buried in new sediment. Their soft parts will quickly decay but their hard parts may form fossils. So animals that live in or near fresh or sea water are more likely to become fossils than those that live in dry uplands.

Some fossils remain in their original state. However, if suitable chemicals are present in the water and sediment, then the fossils may become hardened or the animals may be dissolved away to form *moulds* or *casts*.

Replacement

Over millions of years, some fossil remains may be dissolved by the chemicals in the water and sediment. Gradually the remains of the animals are replaced with *minerals* which harden to form stone. In many such fossils the minutest details of the creatures are preserved. These solid rock fossils can withstand great pressures and cannot be easily destroyed.

When plants are buried, the soft parts are often replaced by dissolved minerals such as *silica*. These *petrified* remains often show fine detail such as remains of leaves and the annual rings of tree trunks. In some places petrified forests have been uncovered.

A prehistoric reptile dies and falls to the sea bed. The soft parts are eaten or decay away, and the skeleton becomes buried under layers of sediment, which eventually turns to stone. If the sea then retreats or dries up, the fossil remains of the creature may be exposed.

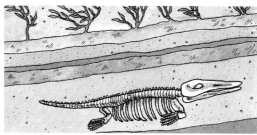

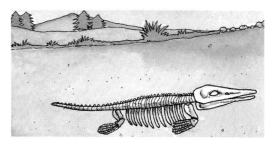

Permineralization

The hard shells and bones of animals contain many tiny holes or pores. Minerals from the water and sediment seep into these pores and harden to form stone. The *permineralized* fossils look the same as the originals, but they are heavier and less fragile.

Moulds and casts

If the remains of plants and animals are dissolved away, only an impression, or mould, of the organism is left. This mould may become filled with minerals, which harden into stone and form a cast. Moulds and casts only show the external details of the organism, none of the internal structure is preserved.

Sometimes water and chemicals soaking through the rock dissolve away an animal's remains. This leaves a natural mould showing just the fossil's outline.

The mould left by a creature that has completely decayed may fill with mud. If this turns to rock it forms a natural cast, an exact replica of the animal.

Some fossils are not the remains of animals themselves, but are traces of them. They may be footprints, droppings or marks made while they were feeding. What do you think made this footprint?

Other fossil forms

Occasionally whole animals, including their internal organs, are preserved as fossils. A woolly mammoth was found in Siberia perfectly preserved in frozen mud. More commonly, insects preserved in amber have been found. The insects which landed on the sap, or resin, oozing from a tree became trapped. Gradually, over millions of years, the resin turned into clear, golden amber with the insect perfectly preserved in its centre.

Some fossil remains, especially plants and graptolites, are converted into carbon films by a process called *carbonization*. These films, trapped in rocks, show the shape of the plant or animal, often in great detail.

Sometimes sediments fill the hollows made by footprints, burrows or worm casts and turn into rock. Such *trace fossils*, including animal droppings, can tell *palaeontologists* a lot about the way of life of the animals.

RECORD OF THE ROCKS

The Earth probably formed over 4,600 million years ago, and life evolved more than 3,500 million years ago. The oldest known fossils are 3,100 million years old. But there are no fossils of the first organisms because they were microscopic and soft-bodied.

Geologists, who study rocks, and palaeontologists, the fossil experts, have divided the earth's history into a number of divisions called eras and periods. Particular periods are associated with different animals and plants. Using your general knowledge and the geological time scale pictured below, see if you can answer the questions in the Project.

Era	Period	Epoch Millions of years ago	Major plants and animals	
Cenozoic	Quaternary	Recent	Modern man emerged	
		0·01		
		Pleistocene	Many 'woolly' mammals; coming of Ice Age in North	
		1·8		
	Tertiary	Pliocene	'Apemen', many large mammals died out	
		6		
		Miocene	Apes, mammals multiplied	
		22·5		
		Oligocene	Early apes, modern mammals, many flowering plants	
		38		
		Eocene	Early horses, modern plants	
		55		
		Palaeocene	Mammals flourished	
		65		
Mesozoic	Cretaceous		Flowering plants; ammonites, large reptiles, dinosaurs died out	
		141		
	Jurassic		Flying reptiles, first birds, many dinosaurs	
		195		
	Triassic		First dinosaurs, first mammals, many ammonites, forests	
		230		
Palaeozoic	Permian		Trilobites died out; first trees	
		280		
	Carboniferous		First reptiles, clubmosses, ferns, horsetails	
		345		
	Devonian		Many fish, first amphibians, land plants, insects multiply	
		395		
	Silurian		Armoured fish, first land plants, insects	
		435		
	Ordovician		First fish, trilobites, echinoderms, brachiopods	
		500		
	Cambrian		Graptolites, trilobites, shellfish	
		570		
	Precambrian	from 4,600		

SCIENCE PROJECT

1. Which era do you think is called the Age of Dinosaurs?

2. When did the first mammals arise?

3. When did the first backboned animals emerge onto land? What kind of animals were they?

4. What were the first backboned animals that could live totally on land? When did they evolve?

5. How long ago and in what period did the first fish arise?

6. Which large group of land animals died out at the end of the Cretaceous period? How long ago was this?

7. How long ago and in which period did the first land plants evolve?

8. What is the age of the rocks in which you would find the first dinosaurs?

9. Which large group of animals rapidly increased in number after the dinosaurs died out?

10. How long ago and in which period did flowering plants arise?

Answers
1. Mesozoic; **2.** Triassic; **3.** Devonian; Amphibians; **4.** Reptiles; Carboniferous; **5.** 435 to 500 million years ago; **6.** Dinosaurs; 65 million years ago; **7.** About 400 million years ago; Silurian; **8.** 195 to 230 million years old; **9.** Mammals; **10.** 65 to 140 million years ago; Cretaceous.

SCIENCE FACTFILE

▶ Fossil records

Some plants and animals only survived on Earth for a relatively short time. So, their fossil remains are only found in one particular layer of rock. They are called *index fossils*. If the same kind of index fossil is found in two layers of rock some distance apart, then those layers were formed at the same time.

Some ammonites, such as the Cretaceous *Hoplites* or Jurassic *Promicroceras*, and trilobites, such as the Cambrian *Cedaria*, are good index fossils. These animals changed rapidly over a short time but are common, widely-distributed fossils. Fossil graptolites, which exist only in Palaeozoic rocks, are also excellent index fossils as each species only lived for a short period of time.

A geological map of your area will show you where the various rock types are found, and in what geological period they were formed. But the rocks are not usually on the surface. They are covered by a top layer of earth, and will only be exposed at quarries and cliffs. This is where you may find fossils.

Cuttings for new roads, river banks, and other *excavations* can also expose fossil-bearing rocks.

Probably the easiest, and the best, place to look is at sea cliffs. The debris at the bottom of the cliff may provide numerous specimens, but do not hammer at cliff faces, or climb anywhere that could be dangerous.

Your local library may have information on local fossil sites. Better still, if you have a local museum or geological society they may be able to tell you where to search.

PROJECT 1

The fossil hunt

Some fossils have been moved far from the rock formation in which they formed. Sometimes this is by natural processes, sometimes by the actions of people. If you keep your eyes open, you can find fossils in surprising places. It can be interesting to trace the history of these fossils.

STEP 1

Study your local geological map. It will show villages, roads and the contour lines, marked in black. Sometimes a cross-section of the area is given, which shows the hills, plains and valleys. The key to the map will show the age of the rocks. It will help you to find possible sources of fossil-bearing rocks in your area.

A geological map

This shows how the land forms hills and valleys

Key

Triassic clays and mud-stones	
claystone	
siltstone	Lower Jurassic
sandstone	
limestone	Upper Jurassic
limestone	

60 80 100 140 160 180 200 120 180 160 150

14

STEP 2

Fossils may be found in apparently unlikely places like a shingle beach. Many of the beach pebbles are made of flint, which can contain remains of sponges, sea urchin spines and so on. Next time you are throwing pebbles in the sea, look at them first. Do any contain fossils?

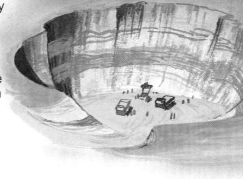

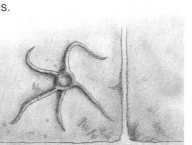

STEP 3

Fossils may be found in towns. Some kinds of building stone contain fossils. Can you spot any in the buildings around you? In some towns, museums have 'geological trail' leaflets which may help guide you to some sites.

STEP 5

Make a scrapbook of your findings. You could make a map showing where your fossil was found. Draw a picture of the fossil then find out what it looked like in real life and draw a picture of that. Write down the date it lived, what it may have eaten and any other information you can find out.

STEP 4

If you discover an 'out of place' fossil, try to find out where it came from. Is the pebble on the beach of a kind found fairly close by, or has it been carried many kilometres by wave action? Is the building stone from a local quarry, or has it been brought a great distance, perhaps even from another country?

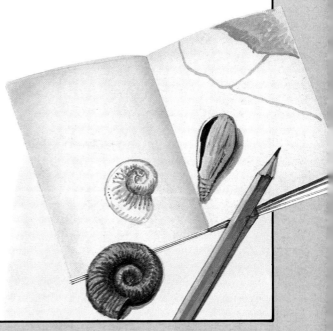

EVOLUTION

The Universe probably began with a great explosion of gases. These gases slowly cooled and condensed to form the planets and the Sun. As the Earth cooled, various chemicals formed and these reacted together to form new substances. Some of these chemicals dissolved in the warm seas and lakes forming a rich 'primeval soup'. It was from these chemicals that life formed.

The first living things were simple single-celled organisms. Gradually, over thousands of years, these developed into blue-green algae, the first life forms to leave fossil evidence. Organisms continued to evolve from this primitive beginning until at the start of the Cambrian period, about 570 million years ago, many forms of life flourished in the sea. Fossil evidence suggests that most of the major invertebrate groups (animals without backbones) developed during this period. Some of these slowly changed into present-day forms.

Life invaded the land about 420 million years ago when the first land plants developed. At this time fish, from which amphibians evolved, were also abundant. The first true land animals, reptiles, arose in the Carboniferous. One branch gave rise to the dinosaurs, which ruled the land until their extinction at the end of the Cretaceous. Dinosaur 'graveyards' containing dozens of fossils have been unearthed. Mammals evolved rapidly after the death of the dinosaurs and eventually, about 10,000 years ago, modern man emerged.

The number of different species gradually increased until they reached the variety seen today. Fossils allow us to trace the paths by which animals

and plants developed into their present forms. Some such as horseshoe crabs, mayflies and nautilus have changed little since they first arose. Others, like elephants and horses, have changed a great deal. Some species have died out completely, and are known only by their fossil remains.

TYPES OF FOSSILS

Most fossils are the remains of just the hard parts of animals. Shells fossilize well. So do bones. Hard parts of plants, such as wood or seeds, may also be preserved. Soft parts of animals usually rot after death, or may be eaten by scavengers, so it is very rare to find evidence of skins, stomachs and other organs. Some animals, like jellyfishes and worms, have no hard parts and so are hardly ever fossilized.

In the more 'recent' fossils, which have been buried a comparatively short time, the original bone or shell may still be there. In those that have been buried a long time the original material has usually changed. Minerals have seeped in and hardened the bone, or may have replaced it entirely, although the structure has been preserved. A bone may have turned into silica or a leaf into a carbon film.

Some of the main types of animal and plant fossils found are listed below. The parts of their bodies most often preserved are also given.

Sponges   These are a simple kind of sea-living animal. They are cylinder or vase-shaped with a hole in the centre and many pores on the surface. Fossils of sponges may be found in flint or limestones. They have existed since Precambrian times.

Bryozoans   These tiny sea animals live in colonies and have existed from the Ordovician period. They are often found on the shells of fossilized sea-urchins and mussels.

Graptolites   These are colonies of small animals that floated in the sea. Their fossils exist only in Palaeozoic rocks, and are excellent index fossils.

Worms   Soft-bodied worms rarely form fossils, but the burrows in which they lived are often well preserved.

Coelenterates   Corals and jellyfish belong to this group. They have existed since the Precambrian period. Corals are often found as fossils in limestones.

Molluscs   Fossil molluscs like snails, mussels and squids, are found from the Cambrian period onwards. Some groups, such as true ammonites, were highly successful during the Mesozoic era, but are now extinct.

Brachiopods   These creatures, sometimes called lamp-shells, have a double shell like a clam. They are common fossils in Ordovician rocks.

Arthropods   Insects, spiders and similar animals with jointed legs belong to this group. Many are very delicate so are rarely found as fossils, except under special conditions. Trilobites, early sea-living arthropods, are often found as fossils.

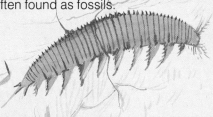

Echinoderms   Sea-urchins, starfish and sea-lilies belong to this group, which has existed since the Cambrian period. Sea-lilies are commonly found in limestone rocks of the Carboniferous period. Sea-urchins occur in later rocks such as those of the Cretaceous period.

Vertebrates   Fish, amphibians, reptiles, including dinosaurs, birds and mammals belong to this group and few of their fossils are found compared to those of other groups. Their bones and teeth are most often preserved.

Plants   These are less common than animal remains, but 'petrified' or preserved forests, remains of stems, leaves or seeds sometimes occur. Coal tips are a good source of plant fossils.

USEFUL FOSSILS

Fossils can be used to reconstruct the history of the Earth and to piece together the mysteries of evolution. They can help determine whether sediments were laid down in shallow or deep seas, in rivers or on land. They are a guide to the geography and ecology of ancient Earth and to the climate. Some fossils are also a source of natural resources which help humans survive.

Fossil fuels

Coal, one of our most important fuels, comes from fossilized trees and plants that grew during the Carboniferous period. Vast swamp forests grew in low-lying areas like mud flats. Much of the land surface slowly sank and the trees were buried beneath mud and sand in the sea water that flooded the forests. The trees became compressed by the weight of sediment above them, and turned into peat. When the sea receded, more forests grew. Often they were flooded again and more peat formed. Gradually the peat hardened and turned to coal. Several seams of coal are often found in such rocks.

Oil is formed from the remains of millions of tiny sea creatures whose remains fell to the sea bed and were covered by silt. Gradually layers of sediment built up and compressed these decaying animals. Eventually, over millions of years, they were changed into oil. Deposits of natural gas formed from these decaying organisms and are often found above oil reserves.

Fossil rocks

Limestone and chalk are formed almost entirely from the fossil remains

Imprints of stems, leaves and bark may sometimes be seen on the flat surfaces of coal or on the shale which is found nearby.

SCIENCE PROJECT

Fossil in amber

Fossilized amber is sometimes used to make jewellery and insects fossilized in amber are highly prized both as fossils and for their beauty. You can make your own fossil in amber. If you make a small one you could wear it on a chain or a large one could be used as a paperweight.

You will need a hobby kit containing embedding resin. The kit will contain resin, a chemical to harden it, and moulds of various shapes and sizes.

1. Mix some of the resin with a few drops of hardener and pour it into a mould until it is half full. Leave the resin to set.

2. Put a dead insect, or, if you prefer, a flower, on top of the set resin and pour in another layer of resin mixed with hardener.

3. Let the resin set and then remove the block of resin from the mould. You now have your own fossil preserved in amber.

You could also use this method to protect fragile fossils.

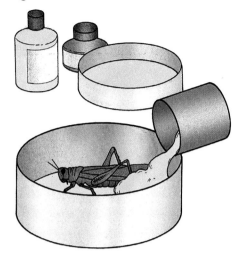

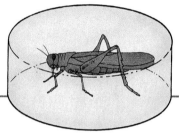

of corals, shells and skeletons of tiny animals. Many of these rocks were formed during the Cretaceous period. Like many other sedimentary rocks, for example sandstone, limestone is used in building. It is also used in cement manufacture and the lime extracted from it is used in the fertilizer and chemical industries.

Ornamental fossils

Fossils are sometimes found in marble, which is metamorphosed limestone. The fossils are unrecognisable as they have been distorted by the heat and pressure that changed the surrounding rock. Amber (fossilized resin) and jet (fossil form of coal) are used as jewellery.

A spider preserved in amber.

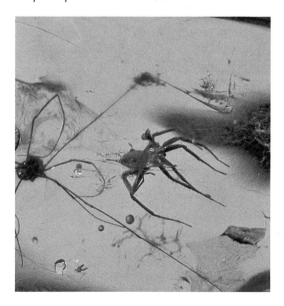

PROJECT · PROJECT · PROJECT · PROJECT · PROJECT · PROJ
ROJECT · PROJECT · PROJECT · PROJECT · PROJECT · PROJE
CT · PROJECT · PROJECT · PROJECT · PROJECT · PROJECT
PROJECT · PROJECT · PROJECT · PROJECT
ECT · PROJECT · PROJECT · PROJECT
PRO
JECT

Tiny fossils are easy to miss in a great mass of rock. But if you are looking for fossils in sands or clays there are ways you can separate the tiny fossils from the rock. Here are two projects which use two different methods.

PROJECT 2

Finding tiny fossils

This project can be done on site, but it may be easier to take a sample of dry sand home and do the project there. You will need two sieves with different sized meshes. You can probably borrow them from the kitchen! Clean them thoroughly afterwards.

STEP 2

Inspect what is left. Is there anything which might be a fossil? Small shells, fish teeth and small bones may be revealed. Try again with the smaller mesh sieve and the same sand – you may discover some even tinier fossils.

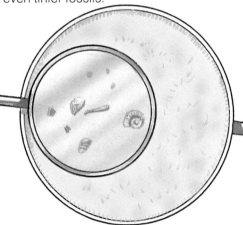

STEP 1

Place some dry sand, which you think may contain fossils, in the sieve with the larger mesh. Shake it gently so that the sand goes through. Any larger items among the grains should be left behind.

Tips – Do not shake too hard – you are trying to find fossils, not break them into pieces. A lens may be useful to inspect what is left in the sieve. (A binocular microscope is even better, if you own or can borrow one.) A small paintbrush may be used to separate your finds from any sand which did not go through the sieve.

PROJECT 3

Baking clay

You can use this method to separate fossils from wet sticky clay which you think may contain fossils. You will need a small baking tin, a bowl, fine mesh sieves and some water.

STEP 1

Put a lump of your clay, about the size of a tennis ball, into a small baking tin. Put your clay in the oven on a low setting 150°C, 300°F, Gas Mark 2, and cook for several hours, until the clay is really dry.

STEP 2

Now place the baked clay in a bowl and soak it with water! This alternate drying and wetting will break up the clay into tiny particles.

STEP 3

Wash your clay sample through a sieve with plenty of water. (Make sure you do not clog the kitchen sink with clay.) Examine what is left behind in the sieve for fossils. You may find small shells or fossil seeds.

Tips – Some clays do not break down easily. First try repeating the drying and soaking. If this does not work, ask an adult to help you boil the clay with detergent or washing soda. This can be messy. A shower spray attachment is handy for washing clay through the sieve.

FOSSIL HUNTING

Fossil hunting and collecting is enjoyed by people of all ages. It combines the excitement of searches and discoveries with the pleasure of being outdoors. For many people finding a well-preserved or unusual specimen is worth many hours of searching.

Secretly, perhaps, many collectors are hoping they will discover a new kind of fossil, or unearth a really spectacular fossil like the skeleton of a dinosaur. Unfortunately, few of us will ever be lucky enough to do that.

Collecting fossils can be more interesting if you have a goal. You might try to get as complete a collection as possible from a certain area or type of rock. You might try to find an example of each major fossil group, or from each main period of the Earth's history. Or you might decide to specialize in, say, ammonites, and become an expert on all the different kinds.

If you collect fossils do not be greedy. A few good specimens are probably all you need. Also, take care not to spoil a site for others by over-collecting or breaking it up.

Professional fossil collectors usually have a target when they work. They set out to find fossils that will answer particular questions. Some fossils are very useful. They may show that rocks are of a particular age or of a particular type. This may mean that oil or gas is to be found nearby. Some microscopic fossils are especially good for this, and geologists from oil companies look out

for them. Another useful type of fossil is coal, the crushed remains of swamp forests that were living about 300 million years ago.

The dinosaur **Baryonyx** was discovered in England in 1983 by an amateur fossil collector, Bill Walker. He found its massive claw bone which is 31cm long. Professionals from the British Museum of Natural History excavated many other bones of the same animal.

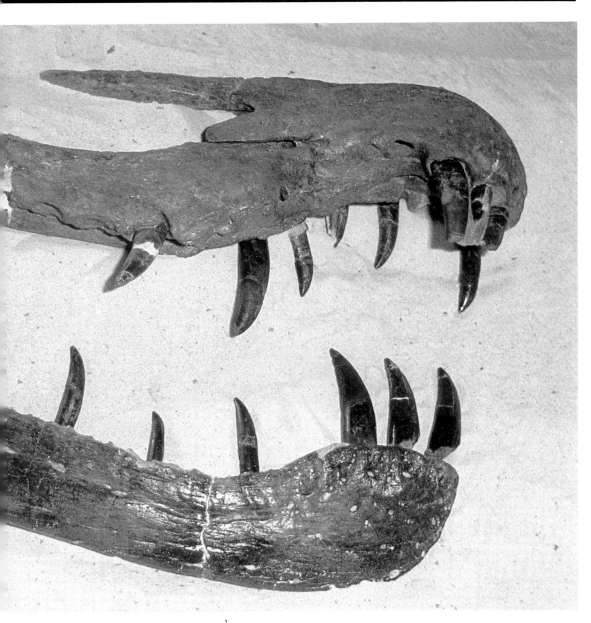

For professional fossil collectors, the real work begins once the fossils have been *excavated* and transported back to the museum. The bones have to be cleaned, sorted out and compared with other similar fossil remains. Then the slow task of recreating the skeleton of the animal begins.

COLLECTING FOSSILS

Fossil collecting is an absorbing hobby. Before you start, you will need to know the local geology of the area you are studying (see page 14), and the sites where the rocks are exposed. You will also need some equipment.

Collector's kit

You will need a basic kit before you can set out on fossil-hunting expeditions. A rucksack or collecting bag is essential. You will also need polythene bags, those with white labels on them are ideal, and sandwich boxes to put your small fossils in. Cotton wool or newspaper can be used to protect them. Larger items can be wrapped in paper and tied with string.

A hand lens is useful for looking at small fossils or details of larger ones. A tape measure, a geological map of the area, a notebook to record your finds and labels to mark them are all useful items. Try to photograph or draw the fossil where it is, but always put a ruler or coin in the picture to show the relative size. To extract the fossils you may need a chisel and geological hammer.

Observing fossils

Look carefully at any fossil you find and sketch it before you attempt to remove it. See which layers of rock it came from, and find out the type and age of the rock if you can. See if you can identify the type of animal it was. Is the fossil on its own? Is it whole? Are there several of them

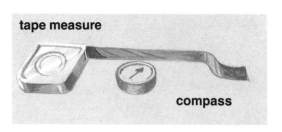

tape measure

compass

notebook

goggles

trowel

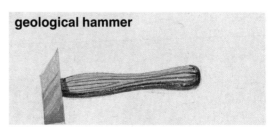

geological hammer

A basic fossil-collecting kit.

lying at the same angle? If so, perhaps they died and were preserved in the place where they lived. This is called a *life assemblage*. Fossil finds like this tell palaeontologists a great deal about the lifestyle of the group.

Perhaps the fossils in the layer you are searching are all broken and jumbled. If they are, perhaps they died elsewhere and were swept away by water currents before being covered by sediments and fossilized. Such a find is called a *death assemblage*.

When you draw or photograph a fossil, always put some kind of measure in the picture to show the relative size.

Extracting a fossil is slow, careful work and it is essential that you label the finds immediately to avoid confusion.

Extracting fossils

Old knives or flat trowels are good tools for getting fossils out of soft rocks like clays and sands. Soft paint brushes are good for clearing away debris. A geological hammer may be needed to extract fossils from hard rocks. They come in all sizes, but one about 1 kg in weight is a good general purpose tool.

Be careful when hammering or chiselling rocks; always wear safety goggles. Never just hammer at the rock, or you will break the fossil. Try to locate the bedding planes, the lines between the different layers of sediment, and break the rocks along these lines.

Sometimes fossils are found which are so fragile that they need special treatment. Fragile fossils are best left in the rock in which they were preserved. Others can be protected by painting them with shellac or a similar varnish. A wood-working adhesive dissolved in water can be used on damp specimens.

CLEANING FOSSILS

Very often you will need to clean or remove rock from the fossils you take home. Some of the softer types of rock may be brushed off a fossil. Some kinds of clay will wash off. Treat the specimens gently so they do not break or crumble.

Freeing the fossil

Some fossils will be set in harder rocks. These can also be freed from their surroundings with a bit of care. If there is a lot of rock around the fossil it can be trimmed off using a hammer and chisel.

Many palaeontology laboratories use just the same kind of technique. They may also use electric drills, including dentist's drills, and vibrating tools, called vibrotools. But even without any expensive equipment you can still produce a good clean fossil if you take care. Always remember to protect your eyes from flying chips if you are chipping pieces off rock.

If the fossils you collect are very damp, *do not* dry them quickly. They may crack and disintegrate. They are more likely to be preserved if you dry them slowly. If specimens have been collected from the sea shore they may be full of salt. Soak them in fresh water for a few days to remove

Electric tools like small drills can be used to channel out or expose a fossil before it is carefully removed.

Preparing and cleaning fossils is slow work. It can take many hours to clean a fossil like this Antrodemus skull.

the salt, then let them dry. If you do not remove the salt, it may *crystallize* and crack the fossils.

The old meets the new

In addition to traditional methods, many laboratories have specialized apparatus for cleaning fossils. A kind of sand-blaster can be used on some. The fossil is placed in a special chamber, and fine *abrasives* mixed with air under pressure are blasted through a nozzle directed at the fossil. Using this equipment a careful operator can reveal the fine details of the shells of fossils such as sea urchins. Apparatus using *ultrasonics* – strong blasts of high-pitched sound – can also be used to free some fossils from their surrounding rock.

SCIENCE PROJECT

Chiselling a fossil out of a rock

1   Fossils are fragile, so work slowly and with extreme care. It is often easier if you can rest the piece of rock on a cushion – a small bean bag or sandbag would do – to steady it.

2   Use a narrow-headed chisel, not a large one, and do not chip too close to the fossil.

3   When you have trimmed off most of the rock you can switch to a sharp penknife or dissecting needle (a sharp needle mounted in a handle). The ends of these can be pressed into the surface of the rock to break off little pieces.

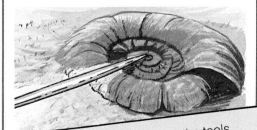

Tip – Do not slide or scrape the tools. They may skid and damage the fossil – or you. (Always take great care when using sharp tools.) Gradually you will clean the fossil from its rock.

CARING FOR YOUR FINDS

Once you have removed and cleaned your fossil finds, you may need to reconstruct them. As most fossils are fragile, they will also need to be protected in various ways. You can do this by varnishing them and by displaying them in a special cabinet or box.

Assembling your fossils

Some of your fossils may be broken, or you may only have small pieces of a fossil. You should study the form and shape of similar animals so that you know how to reconstruct your fossil. You can use modelling clay to make the missing pieces or to fill in small gaps or holes.

If your fossil is cracked or broken, you can mend it with a safe, waterproof glue. However, this will only give a temporary joint and is only suitable for small fossils. If you want a permanent joint, or the fossil is large, ask an adult to help you mend your specimen with a plastic epoxy resin glue.

Crumbling fossils

If you think a fossil is likely to crumble you should paint it with a varnish before storage. Fragile specimens may be given protection by *embedding* them in clear plastic (see page 21). Some fossils look good displayed in this way, but of course you can no longer get very close to their surface for study.

Once you have reconstructed and protected your fossils, you will want to display them. You can buy a display

SCIENCE IN ACTION

Museums transport large fragile specimens wrapped in a plaster bandage for transport. The specimen is covered in wet paper, and then strips of bandage soaked in plaster of Paris are smoothed over, in several layers. When these have hardened, the specimen can be turned over and treated on the underside, or the whole block of rock may be carried away. The specimen is cut out later. This method has been made easier by the use of a lighter material, polyurethane foam.

SCIENCE PROJECT

Fossil protection

Pyrites decay seems to be caused by the action of bacteria. This decay can be prevented by various treatments. Firstly, you should wash your specimen to get rid of any salt. Then you should soak your fossil in an antiseptic, germ-killing solution for five to ten minutes. Allow the fossil to drip-dry slowly. This treatment will help prevent the pyrites from decaying. You could also paint your fossil with clear varnish to seal it off from the air and help protect it.

cabinet, but you could also use a box or similar container. Whatever you use, you should always identify and label your fossils. If you cannot identify a particular specimen from your books, ask at your local museum. The curator will usually be able to help you identify a specimen.

The problem of pyrites

A problem that bothers many fossil collectors is pyrites decay. A number of fossils are composed of iron pyrites, a mineral which can have a shiny golden appearance. (It is called 'fool's gold'.) The fossils often look very beautiful.

Some fossils remain this way, but in others the pyrites breaks down and crumbles away to powder when exposed to the air. This usually occurs slowly over a number of years. There seems to be no sure way of completely stopping the process, but there are ways of slowing it down, some of which are shown in the project.

Caring for your finds begins when you first start to excavate them. Fragile fossils should be handled carefully and their position in relation to each other noted.

FALSE FOSSILS

Some rock formations can look remarkably like fossils. They are called pseudofossils. They often look like parts of plants and animals and can easily mislead the amateur fossil hunter. However, they never have the detailed structure shown by true fossils, and they are often found in unsuitable places or in rocks that do not normally contain fossils.

Flint nodules and clay 'fossils'

Round lumps, or nodules, of chalk and flint sometimes contain fossils. However, if you break a flint nodule open, the ripple marks caused by the fracture lines may look like a trilobite. Lumps of clay that have shrunk as

The pattern of the dried clay inside a septarian nodule can often look like a fossil.

SCIENCE DISCOVERY

Hoax fossils

Not all false fossils are natural, some are man-made. When people first started to study fossils, their limited knowledge made it easy for practical jokers to invent fossils. In 1724, fake clay models of supposedly primitive amphibia and invertebrates confused one professor for many years. In 1846, many great scientists were completely fooled by the fossilized skeleton of a 'sea-serpent'. It was put together by a hoaxer from the fossil bones of a whale!

Perhaps the most famous hoax of all is the story of Piltdown Man. An ape-like jaw and parts of a man-like skull were unearthed in 1912 by Charles Dawson. It was thought to be the 'missing link' in the evolution of man from the apes. However, in 1953 tests proved

that the skull was only a few hundred years old and the jaw belonged to an orang-utan.

they dried, called septarian nodules, often have patterns or marks in them made from calcite. These are often mistaken for fossil twigs or insects.

'Mineral' fossils

Usually when mineral deposits are laid down they form crystals with straight edges. Sometimes, however, they form lumpy, rounded shapes which look like the fossilized remains of animals. Iron ore, known as kidney ore, often forms shapes like this.

Dendrites

Mineral deposits left by water seeping through cracks in rocks often look like the remains of prehistoric ferns or plants. These are called dendrites. Rocks, called moss agates, which are often polished as semi-precious stones, contain dendrites, not fossilized moss.

The mineral deposits left by manganese dioxide seeping through this fine siltstone look like fossil ferns.

SCIENCE PROJECT

Making a cast fossil from a mould

You will need either a natural mould of a fossil, or you can make a mould by pressing a shell or bone into a thick piece of modelling clay to make a deep depression.

1. Paint the inside of the mould with clear varnish to protect it.

2. Build a 'dam' around the mould with modelling clay.

3. Mix some plaster of Paris with a little water to make a thick liquid paste, or use commercial embedding resin plus hardener. Carefully pour the plaster of Paris or plastic resin into the mould until it reaches the top of the plasticine 'dam'. When the plaster or resin is set, remove the dam. The plaster or resin cast is now ready to be lifted carefully from the mould.

4. Carefully remove the cast from the mould. The surface of the plaster or plastic resin cast should show all the details of the original fossil or shell impression.

PROJECT 4

Making a cast 'fossil'

As well as making a cast fossil from a mould, you can make one from a complete fossil. For this you will need a fossil, modelling clay, an old plastic or foil container like a margarine tub, an old mug, plaster of Paris and talcum powder.

STEP 1

Either use one of your fossils, or a present day shell, bone or tooth, or make a replica with modelling clay.

91-108

STEP 2

Fill the mug two-thirds full of water. Carefully add plaster of Paris to the water to make a thick liquid paste. Pour the plaster of Paris into the plastic or foil container until it is half full. Before it sets, press your fossil into it.

STEP 3

Roll out the modelling clay into thin strips. Place the strips of clay so that they touch the edge of the container and fit closely around your fossil.

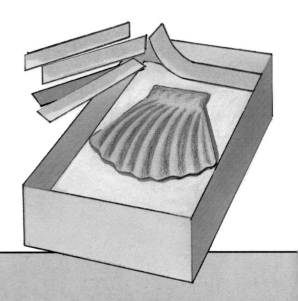

34

STEP 4

Mix some more plaster of Paris and pour it into the container. Make sure that it covers your model. Leave it to set.

STEP 6

Knead some self-hardening or ordinary modelling clay into a soft mass the size of the fossil shape. Press it into one half of the mould. Press the other half of the mould on top, so that the two halves of the mould meet.

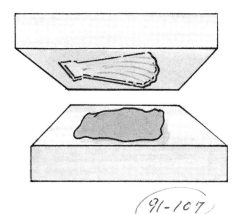

91-107

STEP 5

When the plaster of Paris is hard, remove the whole block of plaster from the container. Separate the two halves and peel away the modelling clay. Take care to clean the clay out of the fossil mould. Remove the fossil. Dust the inside surface of each half of the fossil shape with talcum powder.

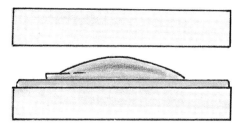

STEP 7

Carefully open the two halves of the mould and take out your fossil cast. Trim the edges. Let it set if you have used self-hardening clay. You now have your own cast 'fossil'.

PUZZLE TIME

Most people who collect fossils like to imagine what the plants and animals looked like when they were alive. Palaeontologists also like to make the remains they find as complete and lifelike as possible, especially if they are going to be displayed in a museum.

Sometimes reconstructing a fossil is just like doing a difficult 3-dimensional jigsaw puzzle. A shell or bone may be in dozens of fragments which need to be sorted and glued together. If a piece of the fossil is missing, the scientist has to guess at its size and shape. This piece is then constructed from a synthetic material, so that the jigsaw can be completed.

With a skeleton, only some of the bones may be there. If a rib or leg bone is missing on just one side it is easy to make a mirror image of the one on the other side. But what if all of both front legs are missing? You may have an idea of how big they should be, but are you right? How many fingers? Did they have long claws or short nails?

Some dinosaur reconstructions you see are based on complete skeletons, and are probably very accurate. Others are guesswork, based on only a few bones, and may or may not be right. When there is a complete dinosaur skeleton it is often possible to see where the muscles were attached to the bone, and this can tell you a great deal about their size and shape. You may find similar marks on the inside of

the shells of fossil *bivalve* molluscs like mussels. They are left by the muscles that held the two halves of the shell closed.

There are some things which we can never find out about fossils. It is very rare for any of the soft tissues to remain. Usually only the hard parts are fossilized. In only a tiny number can we see any sign of what colour they were. We can only guess at the colours of most shells or of dinosaur skins.

THE GUESSING GAME

How can we tell what extinct animals looked like? Usually we can get some idea by comparing the extinct animal with something which is alive today. For example, compare a fossil clam with a living one. If they have similar shells and the marks left by the muscles inside the shell are also similar, then it is reasonable to assume that the fossil clam looked very like the present-day clam. In fact, we have no way of proving this. The soft parts of the fossil *could* have been very different from the present-day animal. But it is simplest to assume they were alike.

What lifestyle?

We also assume that animals have always led the same sort of life. If we find fossil hippopotamus bones, we can be fairly sure we are looking at the

---

SCIENCE PROJECT

Plant or meat-eaters?

Here are some teeth and skulls of fossil animals. See if you can tell what kind of food they ate.

1. This is the skull of *Brachiosaurus*, a dinosaur from the Jurassic. It has small peg like teeth rather like the front teeth of a giraffe.

2. This skull is of the dinosaur *Ceratosaurus*. Look at its sharp pointed teeth, they are like the canine teeth of a present-day cat or dog.

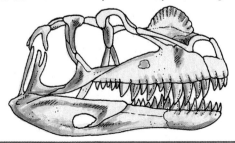

3. These are fossil sharks teeth from the Cretaceous period. They are pointed with saw-edges, and probably pointed backwards as in some of their modern-day counterparts

4. These teeth are flat and chisel-shaped for grinding. They belong to the *Iguanodon*, a dinosaur from the early Cretaceous period. Animals like cows grind up their food.

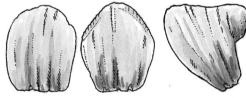

5. This tooth is from a prehistoric fish called *Acrodus*. It has broad flat teeth for crushing.

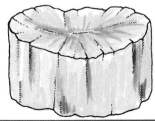

remains of something that lived in water, not an animal that climbed trees or flew. In the same way, if we find fossil corals looking similar to present-day types, we may guess they lived in warm, clear seas, not in freezing muddy ones.

Fossil relatives

The closer a fossil is to something that is living today, the easier it is to guess its lifestyle. But even if a fossil has no living relations, it may still show its lifestyle quite clearly. No plesiosaurs are alive today, but anyone who sees one of these fossil reptiles will know from its flippers and barrel-shaped body that this was a swimming animal.

Many plesiosaur skeletons have long necks and long tails like many land reptiles. But their arm and leg bones are short with long finger and toe bones. These probably had webs of skin attached to them to make flippers, or paddles. Palaeontologists know from this that plesiosaurs lived in the water.

Fossil surprises

Fossil belemnites are commonly found in rocks laid down in seas from 200 to 65 million years ago. All that is found usually is a bullet-shaped shell. This is the skeleton of an animal like a modern cuttlefish or squid. Like a squid, it might have had arms with suckers. A few fossil specimens have been found in which impressions of the soft parts have been preserved. These show that a belemnite did have arms, and even an 'ink-sac' from which it could send out a cloud of ink in defence. What could not have been guessed, without these fossils, was that on some of their arms they had hooks rather than suckers to catch their prey.

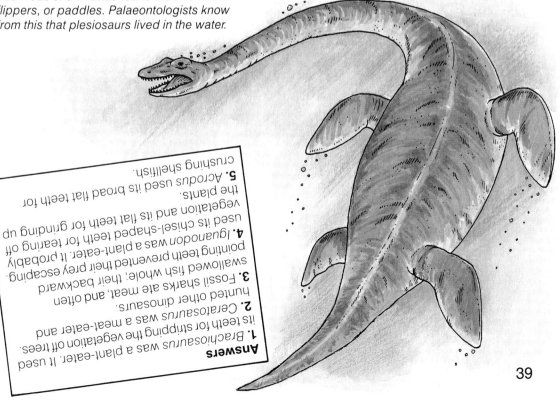

Answers

1. *Brachiosaurus* was a plant-eater. It used its teeth for stripping the vegetation off trees.

2. *Ceratosaurus* was a meat-eater and hunted other dinosaurs.

3. Fossil sharks ate meat, and often swallowed fish whole: their backward pointing teeth prevented their prey escaping.

4. *Iguanodon* was a plant-eater. It probably used its chisel-shaped teeth for tearing off vegetation and its flat teeth for grinding up the plants.

5. *Acrodus* used its broad flat teeth for crushing shellfish.

MYSTERY FOSSILS

For some fossils we can make accurate reconstructions. We can guess what they looked like, what they ate, and even something about their behaviour. But there are some fossils which are not at all easy to understand. Sometimes this is because they have no obvious living relatives, and they themselves give few clues about their lifestyle. An example is *Hallucigenia*, a tiny creature whose remains have been preserved in rocks that are about 530 million years old. It seems to have walked on the sea bottom on seven pairs of pointed spines, and had other 'limbs' sticking out from the top of its body. What it did with them, how it lived, and what its relations are, we just do not know.

SCIENCE IN ACTION

The ammonites

Fossil ammonites are often found in Jurassic and Cretaceous rocks. Most had shells which were a smooth, flat coil. Other kinds have a variety of lumps, spikes or ridges on them. The shell is made up of a series of chambers. But what did these animals look like when they were alive? Did they rest with their shells flat on the bottom? Or did they swim? The 'standard' way of drawing ammonite shells is with the hole at the top. Is this really how they looked?

We can guess at some of the answers because there is still a distant relation of ammonites living, the nautilus of the tropical seas off the coasts of south-east Asia. This, too, has a coiled shell with many chambers. The animal swims, shell uppermost, with the head and arms sticking out of the shell below. Most of the living tissue of the animal is in this last chamber, but a thread of flesh runs up through the middle of each chamber in the shell. Nautilus uses its shell for buoyancy. The chambers have gas in them. The thread of tissue can alter the gas content and therefore the buoyancy.

ammonite

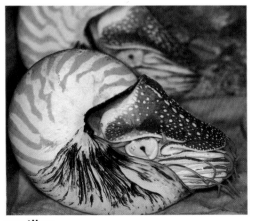

nautilus

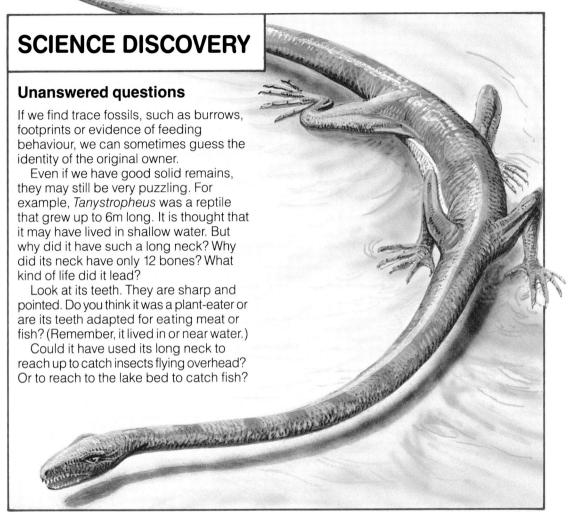

SCIENCE DISCOVERY

Unanswered questions

If we find trace fossils, such as burrows, footprints or evidence of feeding behaviour, we can sometimes guess the identity of the original owner.

Even if we have good solid remains, they may still be very puzzling. For example, *Tanystropheus* was a reptile that grew up to 6m long. It is thought that it may have lived in shallow water. But why did it have such a long neck? Why did its neck have only 12 bones? What kind of life did it lead?

Look at its teeth. They are sharp and pointed. Do you think it was a plant-eater or are its teeth adapted for eating meat or fish? (Remember, it lived in or near water.)

Could it have used its long neck to reach up to catch insects flying overhead? Or to reach to the lake bed to catch fish?

Tiny teeth?

Other fossils are mysteries, because they are just isolated bits, and we cannot be sure what they belong to. Conodonts are microscopic fossils which are found in ancient rocks. They are varied in shape, but look like tiny teeth.

Some scientists think that they belonged to fish or to the ancient relations of snails or crabs. Another suggestion is that they belonged to types of worm.

Different species?

If you find two very similar fossils where the only difference is one of size, you may be looking at the male and female of the species. Pairs of fossil ammonites have been found in which only the shape of the entrance to the shell is different. This may well be a sex difference between the male and female. Similarly, pairs of duck-billed dinosaurs have been unearthed which are the same except that one has a bigger crest.

Do you wonder how experts can state, with confidence, the weight of a particular dinosaur that lived 200 million years ago? This project tells you how they do it and how you can do it yourself. First you will need to find a fossil dinosaur . . .

PROJECT 5

Weighing a dinosaur

If you can't find a fossil dinosaur, a good model will do, provided it is solid. You also need a bowl into which your dinosaur will fit completely. You need another larger bowl, and an accurate measuring jug or another means of measuring water volume (see Tips). You will also need pencil, paper and perhaps a calculator.

STEP 1

Fill the small bowl completely to the brim with water. Stand it in a large empty bowl. Drop your dinosaur into the small bowl and let it sink. As it enters the bowl, water will overflow into the outer bowl.

STEP 2

Measure the amount of water that overflowed in an accurate measuring jug. The volume of the displaced water will be equal to that of the model dinosaur.

STEP 3

Now for some calculations. What scale is your model? If you are not sure, measure its length, and see how many times this will divide into the length of the dinosaur given in a good reference book. This will give the scale, which you must use to work out the volume of the real dinosaur.

STEP 4

For example, suppose the scale is 1 to 30. The height is 30 times that of your model, the length is 30 times, the width is 30 times. So you must multiply the volume of your model by (30 x 30 x 30) to get the volume of the real dinosaur. Reptiles nowadays weigh about 0.9 times as much as their own volume of water. It was probably the same for dinosaurs. So, multiply your answer by 0.9 and you have the dinosaur's weight – in *grams*. Divide by 1,000,000 if you want the answer in tonnes!

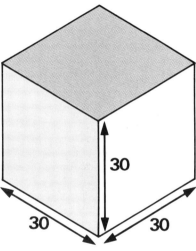

Tips – The model *must* be an accurate one. Suitable models are available at many museums. If you have no other way of measuring volume, you can use a teaspoon or medicine spoon. A standard spoonful of water is 5ml.

THINGS TO REMEMBER

What the words mean....

Here are some explanations of words in this book that you may find unfamiliar. They aren't the exact scientific definitions, because many of these are very complicated, but the descriptions will help you to understand the book.

ABRASIVE A material such as sandpaper, pumice or emery used to clean, smooth and polish a fossil specimen.

BIVALVE A mollusc like a mussel with the shell made up of two hinged halves.

CARBONIZATION The process by which a fossil is formed when only the carbon content of the original tissue remains.

CAST A solid object that shows the shape of the fossil animal. Natural casts form when a mould is filled with minerals.

CRYSTALLIZE To form solid crystals.

DEATH ASSEMBLAGE A mixture of fossil remains deposited together by a storm or flood away from their original surroundings.

EMBED To fix firmly and deeply in a surrounding solid mass.

EVOLUTION The gradual change of the features of a group of living things over successive generations. Eventually the changes are so great that new groups arise.

EXCAVATE To unearth or dig out objects very carefully.

EXTINCT An animal or plant group is extinct when it has died out.

FOSSIL Animal and plant remains from the Earth's distant past.

GEOLOGICAL COLUMN Sequence of rock types and the time scale they represent. Systems of rocks and time periods bear the same name.

GEOLOGIST A person who studies rocks, minerals and their structure.

IGNEOUS ROCKS A type of rock formed from molten matter from below the Earth's surface.

INDEX FOSSILS Fossil animals and plants that only lived for a short time and can therefore be used to work out the age of a particular rock layer.

LAVA Molten rock which is forced out through holes or cracks in the Earth's crust.

LIFE ASSEMBLAGE A mixture of fossils from a single community preserved in their original surroundings.

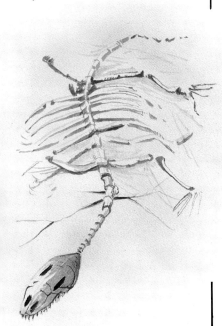

METAMORPHIC ROCKS A type of rock formed from rocks that have been changed by enormous pressure and/or heat.

MINERAL A naturally occurring substance with a characteristic chemical make up.

MOULD A cavity formed when the hard part of an animal is dissolved away leaving an impression in the rock.

PALAEONTOLOGIST A person who studies fossils.

PERMINERALIZATION The way in which a fossil is formed when minerals are deposited in the pores of shells or bones of animals.

PETRIFIED FOSSIL The tissues of an animal or plant are entirely replaced by minerals – turned to stone.

PRESERVE To protect from total destruction and decay.

REPLACEMENT The hard parts of an organism are slowly dissolved and replaced by minerals to produce a stone replica.

SEDIMENT Small particles of matter that collect, layer by layer, in water or on land to form rock.

SEDIMENTARY ROCK A type of rock made from sediment that has built up layer by layer and hardened to form rock.

SILICA A naturally occurring hard glassy material like quartz.

TRACE FOSSIL A fossil that shows the presence of an organism, but is not part of it, e.g. foot prints, worm casts.

ULTRASONIC High-pitched sounds which can be used for various purposes including shaking free fossils from their surroundings.

INDEX